time
being

KUHL HOUSE POETS

edited by Mark Levine and Emily Wilson

# time being

poems

Oni Buchanan

University of Iowa Press, Iowa City

University of Iowa Press, Iowa City 52242
Copyright © 2020 by Oni Buchanan
www.uipress.uiowa.edu
Printed in the United States of America

Text design by Barbara Haines

Printed on acid-free paper

Library of Congress Cataloging-in-Publication Data

Name: Buchanan, Oni, 1975– author.
Title: Time Being / Oni Buchanan.
Description: Iowa City : University of Iowa Press, [2020] | Series: Kuhl
  House Poets
Identifiers: LCCN 2020006565 (print) | LCCN 2020006566 (ebook) | ISBN
  9781609387167 (paperback : acid-free paper) | ISBN 9781609387174 (ebook)
Subjects: LCGFT: Poetry.
Classification: LCC PS3602.U25 T56 2020  (print) | LCC PS3602.U25  (ebook)
  | DDC 811/.6—dc23
LC record available at https://lccn.loc.gov/2020006565
LC ebook record available at https://lccn.loc.gov/2020006566

## Contents

*Voyagers*

Tim Eck | Neil Fidler

*Bedrock*

Robin Welte | Jon Woodward

time
being

## Not to Half-Ass It

The demands of not | half-assing this one
      thing are more | stringent than simply

half-assing 99% of all | the other things The price
      tag not to half- | ass it is near

unbearable The price tag | not to half-ass it
      is objectively | unreasonable What's

a "reasonable" demand | to ask of oneself? When you
      compare the amount | to other amounts

When you make a mortal | ratio of numbers
      The economics | are not on a

human scale The extremity | of it means in a way
      we've reached | the terminal point

of a perception of how | things are supposed to
      play out The | disowned theory

of mimicry Drive to efface | the distinction between
      self and | environment "Instinct

of renunciation" Because if | you were "smart" the
      whole way | being shuttled

along this tunnel being | crammed down this
      excruciating tunnel | you were looking

for a janitorial doorway | leading elsewhere leading
      to a room | with a party piñata

and people half-assing | the beating down of some
representational animal | stubbornly

metaphorical animal | to achieve a low-quality
leak of generic | drugstore candy—

## Factory Tour

We're streaking by a | node One possible
          endpoint | Electrical wires

a magnetized prophecy | flying alongside
          foreseeing the | platform where

we'll disembark with | all our luggage Here we
          are So what's | the factory

of this city The industry | that bends this segment
          of the populace | to its will

Styled in the shape | of the endeavor Bent
          by the priorities | of the endeavor

Choreography of workers | amidst the assembly
          robots their | slender orange

arms mechanized in | perfect synchronization at
          their welding | stations Turbines

to mix the vast liquids | Rollers that grind it out
          to powder | The train

traces taut unflinching | fibers straight through
          the landscape | It's pure

propulsion Silken strands | the ghosts of a lineage
          of operators | Confidential paystubs

quantifying value One | human life working on
          task X for | X hours

## Sotto Voce

I'm driving past Hardscrabble | Rd past Trashdump
    Rd Blessed are | the meek for

they shall inherit | {whatever} Thou shalt not
    covet the wealth | and health insurance

of thy neighbor I've made | a business decision
    to throw a | penny in the

blue-tiled fountain I tore out | the ecosystem by its
    roots and watched | transparent spiders

flee Nothing to see here | Nothing that would interfere
    Is it shouting | all day that persuades

the people? Is it pounding | with one's fist or staging
    a good cry | during prayer circle

that persuades the people? | Friends the gavel the
    gravel is falling | overhead and

scuffing up the windshield | with dirty scrapes and
    streaking Friends | the State Line

got blurred by herds | of white-tailed deer that
    crossed it | silently while

night descended Friends I | backpacked unto your
    living room and | here I pitch

my nylon tent Friends | I caged this cube of suet
    and give me ten | dollars for it

## This Valuable Item

What a merchant's mouth was saying A legal
        pad A trespass Severed
        cables from the hacked-off
        shoulder The blast furnace forging

golden tokens By "regular" I mean
        "maintained" By "astonished" I mean
        "greatly disappointed" The intricate
        intoxicating wrappers pressed and

saved I arrive late to the christening Thank
        God not too late Wooden birds
        nailed to the dry birdbath My marigold
        in a half-pint milk carton cut with

rounded scissors My orphan marigold offered
        depleted dizzying in
        fragrance My punctilious marigold
        hallucinating its bursting My

shivering perfunctory marigold I'm
        dehydrated Thank God this
        valuable item will make me well
        again These drained out colors will

heal me Aromatic essence captured from the
        lingering mists You called me
        back You wrote me back on fine linen
        letterhead Your missive arrived You

responded to my inquiry You liked my posting
in the local circular You said "I hear you
I love what you're saying to me right now I
love what you're saying—"

## Free Market Value

We heard a near bird | this morning "So near!"
      we thought in | unison Tracked

like stutters A series of | bleats Does this increase
      the free market | value of our

property? We're cramped | inside the hovel
      sweeping it out | as best we can

Please give us a reasonable | 300-piece puzzle
      that we might | calm ourselves

with some achievement | Or we could bake
      snickerdoodles | A pizza slice

could be the apex of our | day We could take a
      painting class | All of us in

smocks "accidentally" | smudging paint on our
      hands and sleeves | Why yes I

took a painting class last | evening I took a serious
      beating I mean | we painted

harbor ships at sunset | copied stroke for stroke the
      heavy brushstrokes | of our capable

instructor Here's what we | deny ourselves and here's
      what we deny | each other

## Perfectly Tendered

Are the gaps technical | difficulties or intentional
    virtuosities | At a certain

point you change | unalterably One degree one
    degree until | your trajectory

is irrevocably re-routed | Revisionary history
    Steal it | from me then

offer it back to me | for purchase The ultimate
    "currency conversion" | A perfectly

tendered transaction | Well I've designed
    the screen | A retractable

display that stays | within the confines of my
    designated | exhibition footprint

It's hard to guess the | next misstep Anticipate
    X moves | ahead The sextant

calibrated to a cruel | constellation Tender person
    Who will be | beside you

in the daily moments | Unmeasured moments
    linking found | arrivals linking

downbeats Who will be | with me? This ship deck
    tilted toward | the solitary

## The Masterful Arches

I'm in a sunbeam I'm in a shady bed of clover
       What from here shall be revealed
       What from here will the buzzer make
       What the linen on the line do breeze

I'm in a fecund pile of potting soil
       What from here will the seed do lean
       Will the stem do sway
       Flowers from the uncut grass

On the water line In the aqueduct
       The masterful arches lead and fall away
       The tunnel of thirst the sobbing buzzes
       The stilted lilies the stabbing petals

I crossed a bridge over the deafening
       municipality Panoramic distance
       I raised a coronet to my lips
       The revolutionary loudness of dandelions

I spoke through the live end of a stethoscope
       The sabre hilt The pageant of my
       threadbare sundress How is your heart
       How is the openness of your heart

Behind Glass

So what if it's the opposite of trust Frankly I could
        care less what you think you're about to tell me
        right now Behind glass

So line up all your dead predecessors like candlepins
        without fire that weep without wax I'm the
        machine that sets them up again all their
        featureless faces and neckties

You know for real all these supposed "problems" I just
        want an order of fried pickles I could give a shit
        what you're trying to say to me right now Behind glass

Who's at the negotiation table now I'm going to
        destroy you for this level of bullshit
        No what I'm going to do is incinerate
        you with pure rigorous reason

But what's the LONG game like really HOW LONG
        you would be right to ask All these humans one by
        one just trying to do their best Behind glass

Isolate to get a drop of the essence Sure I understand
        your disappointment I sincerely
        understand it It's no wonder and I literally mean
        there is not one single wonderment left

## The Elites

The flesh burned away | from the body or cut away
      in laminae | and the shape

"self-evidently" revealed | The "ideal" version To
      refine or to be | bent against one's

will To have one's abstract | plea for transformation
      answered by the | brutality required

*Break blow burn and* | *make me new* I saw "The Elites"
      run by Their bodies | were the shape

of their devotion No inch | of excess remained What
      is "practice" | "singularity of desire"

"stripped of other aspiration" | *imprison me* Down to the
      cellular Applauded | as they ran past

by a crowd of everyday | humans undifferentiated for
      excellence All of us | lined up behind

the barrier to witness the | alien lives stride by with
      smooth muscular | strokes *Except you*

*enthrall me* Entirely efficient | mechanized motion In the
      snapshot of those | mere one hundred

yards we saw each approach | exist in front of us and
      pass They | seemed to run

at a pace we could run | Doppler effect of excellence It
      bends into the | moment Is perceived

as achievable *Knock breathe | shine and seek to mend*
        *then bends | away* I could

keep up if I leapt into | the fray Transformation has a
        folded route | of pain "Push

through Put stress on the | body That's how things change
        That's how change | is gonna happen"

says Jillian Michaels in her | "30-Day Shred" You descend
        into eviscerating | pain until your

ratio of excoriated cells | to new cells generated
        through default instinct | for survival

balances The new somehow | exceed They accumulate to
        take some other | shape and you

emerge again unalterably | changed I paid four quarters
        to watch one | penny be flattened

past recognition then re- | imprinted with a beluga whale
        newly minted | on its surface

## Road to Vienna

I was already slightly | perplexed by their ravenous
        deployment of | my name

Placed at intervals like a | hypnotic chime as if
        to ring it | would re-weaponize

my eyes Sometimes | so maniacal it rendered
        like a snarl | Because how

could I make it to the | Annual Viennese Ball
        without their | violating proximity?

And that would cost me | Fortunately my personal
        tragedy and | other details

extracted from me | over the course of introductory
        lessons could | inform their

pitch Well we've created | a package just for you
        that in your | situation you

need now more than ever | An exclusive customized
        offer We've | laboriously printed

and stapled this packet | with a pixelated Hofburg Palace
        cover and | the proclamation

in cursive font: "Road to | Vienna!" This 60-unit package
        is discounted | just for you

payable in smaller increments | But if you hate yourself
        you can choose | instead this

20-unit package In all | likelihood it won't suffice
    to meet your | goal You

almost certainly won't make it | to Vienna You might be
    stranded out | in Klagenfurt—

## Pain Threshold

The body swallows the stitches once the

tethering becomes   redundant *repugnant*

The living tissue all on its own

like a miracle of physical ingenuity

*immunity* There isn't easy solace for this

temper The blank shot straight up

to scare away the vultures Just

casing Vacant epidermis All my

preparation All my learning and

endurance *Convergence* The impossibility

of reaching it through my own

powers my own significant powers I

pummel the surface area till it gives up

the ghost of the inner chamber Whose

receptors are this open *Misspoken* I

have come to understand that my

pain threshold is preternaturally high

To know beforehand would baffle the

very definition Impeached I am

decreed the unsolved daughter fodder

for a lesson received *don't*

*leave don't lessen* *me* I'm only

naively beginning Selecting a clean

leaf for the calligraphy of words

chosen specifically for you Bamboo

brush dipped in lemon juice The

acidic cursive flourish *malnourished*

burns first revealing meaning

before a fire catches All my

sleights of hand *abandoned* Pour this

love into your love then strain it

back to its original          molecules Unfold

the letter back               to its pristine

un-intentioned sheet          A square of sky

## Pain Is a Kind of Information

Ice-lichen on the buttressed rocks The
    oxidized indestructible hull
    of sunken ship The body must be
    warmed in a controlled environment

and even then to return after molecular
    motion ground to a halt? Even one
    degree too quickly would cause
    costly complication Give me

increments Dosages that fit the limits
    of my intake calibrations The dosage
    here is half a cracker The dosage
    is this crust of bread Divided up

divided up again I am circling around
    a wound that is unhealable
    Cauterized in ice Except to leave
    the freezing room Everyone is

fatigued and I am also fatigued Listen
    to your body when it tells you
    I am tired Listen to your body's
    pain Your heart in pain Take

the clue before you Pain is a kind of
    information When your body tells
    you When your heart tells you
    I'm in pain now I'm in pain

## How Heavy

What would be
a necessary shift

What would
enable you enable

me What
would need

to move How
heavy would it

be How intricate
How laced fine

and sinewy the
filigree Woven

deeply to the
core How painful

would it be
How painful *not*

to move that
heavy stone I

move the stone
It is heavy

I do not move
the stone It

is heavy
I do not want

to cause you any
pain Beautiful

creature Most
extravagant creature—

## Prosthetic Mermaid Tails

Prosthetic mermaid tails | for humans are now
    in the queue | of consideration

to be declared illegal | The problem stands that
    when wearing | mermaid tails

humans become fooled by | the temporary physicality
    by the merging | of the legs

into a fin To think that they | could stay underwater
    longer than | is possible

given human limitations | of breathing People were
    drowning! Human | men and women

who wore mermaid tails | found their brains in such
    a state of | underwater ecstasy

Gliding Speeding Diving | deep They lingered
    too long | They engaged

the illusion 10–15 seconds | too long (Approximately)
    Just the slightest | misdemeanor The

slightest self-indulgence The | sheer wonder luxuriating
    at the joy | the sudden

intoxicating quantity of bliss | and freedom And snapping to
    found themselves | deep in an

uninhabitable ecosystem | Suddenly the limits of the
    breath's elasticity | are reached The

surface frames a tantalizing | gateway The sun shines high
    above the | shimmering boundary—

Dear {Salutation} {Last_Name},

I found your name on a website

offering concerts I am writing to you

at a general email address the only one

provided on your website the only result

found after using Google search engine

in several plausible searches hoping this

message might make it to you (50% chance)

hoping you might open this communication (20%

open rate) hoping you might then read it

with an open heart with curiosity and

consider its contents hoping you might consider

{me} for your concert series

(5% considering rate) hoping you might

converse with me and ultimately

invite me to perform for you as part of

{Series_Name} (1% actual booking rate) I

understand the numbers are against me

the odds are against me

but I hold out this flower

to you hoping you will accept

this long-stemmed flower and

grant me a few words and

not let the hope you give to me

be a vain hope

Receiving Channels

To drink miso soup from a lacquered

bowl by candlelight before the electric

lightbulb reached Japan Heat

permeates the delicate partition The soup

black in the black bowl The soup

clear in the black bowl Inhale

the oceanic vial dispatched into broth

Steam rises off condensing on the

face Taste the grit of cirrocumulus

clouds A Venn diagram of silhouettes

penumbra and opacity The raised

bowl traces its rim-circumference

on air An etching The liquid volume

shifts against the pith A wing An

alien creature's scapula Touch my

lips Centuries

practice and

elixir evanesces

while intimacy

receiving channels

banners unscroll

discrete fragment

and generations of

refinement The

in near-darkness

magnifies across

Drifting seaweed

each bearing its

of the inscription

## Tinder Event

A wild night run in the howling preamble

to a hurricane Alone I turned along the beach Mute

with wind roaring in off the ocean It hurled

sand against my cheek Trash in an ankle-cyclone

tangling my feet I vaulted beach debris

I leapt white gates of bramble-reaches

uprooted from the scrub The ocean only

fury outside language Incoherent

syllables rising from the stench

whipped against my face Pulverized

claws No one out at all Just some cars pulled up

facing the dark now lashed with white

tumultuous waves Frothy mutiny incoming

to crumble at the seam Silence pressed up against

silence in the midst of a roar daring me to speak

# Maximum Absolution

The periodic crescendo

long loop a liquid

stinking on the sand

deserted by a wave

by gulls above the

baking in a sun-tangle

open freed from

minutes the tea-

of days So much

fury and fire! I

down now! I

the maximum absolution

stripping down to the

by fire by discipline

holiness of the task

into breaking The

timekeeper Rack line

Dismembered crabs

Mussels pried open

rocky shore Algae

My body is broken

the regimen of

timers the calendar

maintenance! So much

did it! I've got it

accomplished the thing

the total purge the

studs I'm purified

by my labors by the

I'm cleansed! I'm

cleaned out! I've
scrubbed myself down

whittled past scars
My passion brought me

to the marrow the
meristem to my

knees and now it's
done and here I am

the sun pours in I'm
a hull of myself I'm

free I'm sea glass
from a passing ship

## Unbalances the Fulcrum

The mud flats a

overlaid The weight

*ambivalences* the

to the igneous

model specimen An

sparks are spewed

*injections* Slow down

blue sky balances

equation but our

crooked in all

is illuminated

light that has traveled

seconds to arrive

fragrance *vagrants* At

latches like shutters

momentary rhythm

of a housefly unbalances

fulcrum Straight-pinned

rock formation A

epitome *Pity me* The

in all directions

the rock slide The

both sides of the

shifting gaze makes it

directions Your face

*remunerated* by

X minutes X

A saturated

night your face

*shudders* in all

directions The family
Phylliidae: insects

that engage in
cannibalism when they

mistake each other
for leaves *Bereaves*

Mimicry adaptation
over-achieved The

laugh-particles interpolated
in an otherwise face-

value communication
inject the necessary

flotation for unspoken
persuasive syllables

Complicit the listener
enacts the speaker's

innuendo Desired
action *Infraction*

## Destination City

Running I find the gap in the chain link fence

shutting down the Heritage Trail and duck under

entering its sullied history We all want to be

in a "destination city" not these square allocations

of croplands Not the seedy casinos along what used to be

the Missouri River Pioneer Highway Do I have a gun?

is what the woman in the elevator asked me as I set out

for my morning run along the water I don't know Does the bridge

over the fetid river that divides two states have love-locks

fastened to its railing? With the keys tossed into

the polluted tar-skimmed water swallowing the whole

of light shone to it the whole of sound sung to it Oh hopeful

lovers It's a gap that exists already in the present

moment The water pries its lockjaw open and gullets

the promise Stunted tributaries leading nowhere

## As Ever

I hope the {FLOWERS} is going well for you so far

I hope the first few weeks of {FLOWERS} are going well for you

How is your {FLOWERS} progressing so far

It looks like you have a really exciting {FLOWERS} ahead of you

I took a look at your {FLOWERS} what a great line-up

I wanted to catch you before the busy {FLOWERS} hits

The {FLOWERS} is upon us

I can't believe it's already {FLOWERS}

I wanted to catch you before the {FLOWERS} gets fully underway

It's that time of year again {FLOWERS}

What are you working on for next {FLOWERS}

Do any of them fit what you have in mind for the overarching theme of your next {FLOWERS}

Are you emphasizing {FLOWERS} in your upcoming {FLOWERS}

Are you still planning your coming {FLOWERS}

Are they still under consideration for your coming {FLOWERS}

Have you already wrapped up your decisions for next {FLOWERS}

Are you already looking ahead to the following {FLOWERS}

What is your planning timeline for next {FLOWERS}

May I send you updated materials for next {FLOWERS}

Will {FLOWERS} be exploring the theme of {FLOWERS} again next {FLOWERS}

We really enjoyed working with you last {FLOWERS}

I know he/she/they would love to return in a future {FLOWERS}

Your {FLOWERS} is so courageous in its mission to {FLOWERS}

Thank you for keeping him/her/them/it in mind for next {FLOWERS}

I look forward to working with you next {FLOWERS}

Sincerely My best Best All best All the best Very best Best to you Best wishes to you Best wishes Warm wishes Warmest wishes Warmly Fondly Cordially Cheers Regards Warm regards Best regards Kind regards Yours Yours truly Yours sincerely Respectfully yours Respectfully With all good wishes With appreciation With gratitude Gratefully Gratefully yours Many thanks Sincere thanks Thanks so much Thank you so much Thank you very much Thanks very much Thanks as always Thank you Thanks Looking forward Till then Till soon See you soon Talk soon Soon As ever

## Contrary Motion

So much risk to find another through-line

The same points of data dropped on

different axes It depends on what

emergencies are happening whether I

can take these hours Whether I can

command these hours And my hold

over the activities! To preside over

the ceremony! I'm sure my only

course of action is to love so many

things Each love another quivering

tether holding a rainbow-colored hot air

balloon to the green hillside And on

occasion un-stake the guard ropes the

ground wires Throw the sand bags over-

board and lift off soaring through the

sky with other

Volumized pigments

fire-driven air

create our skybound

looking down the

on the distant surface

in-flight vessels

Dots of channeled

In aggregate we

melodic line then

counterpoint reflected

of a mountain lake

# Hardened Resins Are Called "Tears"

It turns out when landlords say a space
  is "funky" they mean it is "artsy"
  but also "infested by ants" You told me

my gown was "not so elegant" and all of the
  sudden I had no idea what elegance
  was The damage had already been done

The shame was "unresolved" or "not solved
  again" I hate to bother you When you
  commented on my shimmering threads

did you mean "lamé" or "lame"? Shame in reverse
  is reintroducing a population of solitary
  white wading birds to an inlet or estuary

In German to say "I'm sorry" is "Tut mir leid" or
  "All my unfortunates" "All my solitary
  egrets balanced deadly in the tidewater"

A Nigerian man on a flight to Lagos told me
  "Oni" meant "king" in Nigerian though
  he then modified to "royalty" The Oni

embraces the sword of justice and wears
  a ceremonial cloth soaked with the blood
  of sacrificed men and women "Justice"

like "only the frozen state" or impassive
  objectivity unmoved by liquid tears
  We were incredulous that the other

had also devoted his/her life to "poetry"
        until it turned out in mid-air that he
        meant "poultry" Anyway I'm graying

out another pixel on the grid of my surrender
        The procedure to surgically remove
        necrotic tissue known also as "debridement"

and I am so much debris formerly gathered
        at the site I guess debridement is the
        "antidote" like the opposite of "doting"

"Against excessive love regularly expressed"
        There have to be garments for this So tight
        they create their own psychology Pull your dignity

through the eyehole of the needle All my
        possibilities Just to imagine one is to
        invite it closer "Dote" which also means

"decay of wood" In extracting myrrh the tree bleeds
        a "resin" A value proposition One must wound
        the tree repeatedly to achieve it

## Whoso List

Not speaking the
language Not knowing
the city plan
the grid of
streets the public
transport the currency
Not knowing a
single human If
I am unmanageably
sad If I
will find my
way home Night
*Who list her hunt I put him out*

Tell me again
Communicate it That
I taught you
what it is
The unit of
measurement A "cruelty"
of water I
require one cruelty
of water to
douse this fire
to obliterate this
miracle of fire
*But as for me alas*

Silence mirrors the
internal Excruciating I
have to dig
in Scalpel through
the layers to
excise the festering
to excavate this
pain this unbearable
pain Cavity straight
to the root
If I am
all optimism if
*in vain And graven with diamonds*


It's sudden mandatory
workout time One
"discipline" of water
One discipline to
toast this level
of severity Total
deprivation Either you
can die or
you can do
these 1,000 sit-ups
If I do
these 1,000 sit-ups
*I may no more The vain travail*


There's real danger
in not finding
the words in

time Containers left
out in rain
measuring the fallen
agitation Radio static
You must be
"speechless with love"
If the extant
proof If I
am dreading it
*her fair neck round about*


Is there a
way for me
to see this
objectively Can I
"be curious about
this feeling" One
"curiosity" of water
to buoy this
divine this exultant
feeling You whom
I adore with
all my heart
*though I seem tame*


If I am
witnessing it alone
If the sun
scalds my tears
If it casts
a rainbow over

water Rapturous refraction
Truly it's a
pleasure to meet
you It has
most sincerely been
a distinct pleasure
*of doubt As well as I*

What mythic future-
forecaster Not one
iota of focused
rage I am
my own nonarrival
Monstrance of unresponsive
iconography What's the
ersatz version of
this priceless vanity
You whom I
conscript to solve
an ancient problem
*Yet may I by no means*

My pain in
binding terminology Tethered
wires trapped with
pins Harnessed ligaments
The hammer has
a memory Rebounds
to where its
stroke began The
music rises off

now audible The
body under X
tons of pressure
*I know where is an hind*

So what kind
of eternity Like
postponement till we're
dead? One "casual
neglect" of water
One "cosmic distance"
One "planetary" Your
life-minutes are
worth this much
to me "Mundane"
and "moondance"otherwise
such close relations
*diamonds in letters plain*

Like the rest
who didn't know
Everyone's waiting for
me to act
and I'm waiting
for me too
How many backstitches
will this tattered
garment hold A
playlist for the
pace I train

myself to run
*my wearied mind Draw from the deer*


If I might
not notice in
preservation time If
I'm hostage to
extremes Pinotage specific
to the region
One "imperial" of
water turned to
wine One "punishment"
I know you
experience the same
intensity of feeling
*I am and wild for*


It's a wash
Adrenaline rush of
ruin Transference with
no delivery So
many ways to
misapply a theory
a lifetime guarantee
All or nothing
becomes nothing by
simple overpopulation Slake
your thirst with
this fine goblet
*I leave off therefore*

It's not as
pretty as I'd
hoped I don't
have the control
I need How
can I see
what I should
do and then
not execute Not
be able to
execute Not hold
onto it but
*Fainting I follow*

If I am
all anguish the
attempt to control
anguish causing more
anguish If I
am ashamed How
to live inside
each minute Pure
observation Wonder at
the world One
"wonderment" of water
Wake me but
*Noli me tangere*

If the intake
protocol Calendar of
days that without

you How can
I adjust the
frame of my
perception Supposedly it's
these 36 questions
in this order
that make the
heart-machine lock
in Manchurian candidate
*The vain travail hath wearied me*

If I make
a balanced ask
Inquiry where one
outcome of response
won't push it
past the decimal
Devastate this newly
instituted point-of-
purchase I can't
pry it from
your grip To
float this prospect
*in letters plain There is written*

People lived a
lifetime to get
to this moment
Geologic time Complexity
in a molecule
of water One

"lineage" of water
Drenched to navigate
the difference My
battered unseaworthy vessel
A compass spinning
on one leg
*but as she fleeth afore Fainting I*


How can you
not embrace the
same psychology Reconverge
on some farther
focal plane I'm
filling in approximately
similar pixels where
the image gets
blurry Revert to
pinhole aperture One
"aversion" of standing
water Expect poison
*so sore I am of them*


I understand there's
a chance you
cannot meet me
You're running down
this mortal clock
How can I
unteach my cells
such radical diminishment
Will it fall

into place more
beautifully than I
could have imagined
*for Caesar's I am*


How desirable would
it be to
privilege this over
To "hold this
lightly" One "privilege"
of water I
begin with abandonment
I have to
live with the
knowledge you chose
not to rise
to the occasion
*as well as I may spend his time*


To achieve the
skill set blossom-
scatter fluency the
writ cadenza Improvisation
a voluntary reaction
expanded upon indefinitely
What's the value-
add Rebranding in
advance of their
perception A speedy
hedonism loyal to

no other life
*And wild for to hold*


The taste of
this exact sip
of tea We
are immersed in
the problem as
in the elegance
of the solution
Courtesy or base
peasantry I can
barely prevent myself
from justifying any
course of action
*that farthest cometh behind*


If I can
choose the shifting
degrees Let me
nock the arrow
draw the bowstring
to its anchor
point What's dignity
What's grief Tension
and release You
misled me but
clearly I offered
the wrong impression
*Whoso list to hunt*

Forge the breach
by rope-lashed
logs Is my
self-fulfilling prophecy
more tenacious than
your self-fulfilling
prophecy If I
am all flotation
Sun-soaked blue
chaotic streamers offer
radiant transmission Evidencing
ribbons in air
*Since in a net I seek to hold the wind*

## Finite Number

The endgame is

not waterproof not

heavy water

numb Counting out

from land Petrels

finite number a conclusive

the coming moment

to make something

My blood stream

distinguish water from

mix Now is

plunge into the ocean

wake up here bobbing

staring as usual with

the data in their

unflattering My phone's

ringing I'm treading

growing more and more

the sea birds this far

Puffins You arrive at a

number You extrapolate

while losing your means

of that hard-won data

slowing How can I

sky? The silver boundaries

the time novice pilots

I didn't mean to

with harbor seals

no discretion They keep

silver brains insulated

like a coin collection

Byzantine I have to

I've been seeking

to imagine under the

soon black out Float

sky before it hits

all my declines

silver under all this

No hard feelings No

5th- and 6th-century

believe I'm the person

It's easier and harder

severity of pressure I'll

away from this failing

the pitch Now to re-set

before the water ages

barometric pressure

difficult feelings

## Alive and Still

It's so impossible to believe it's

winding down to this A number

of minutes passing The aperture

will click We try to slow it down hoist

a rock in water We try the tide pools

pocked with closed anemones We enter

through the garden path of pollarded

mulberry knotted at the wound

We were sitting in the same room

We were sitting in different rooms

of the same house One of us was in

the house and one in the garden One

was doing yardwork and the other

driving into town We're here

breathing We're alive and still have

bodies maneuvering through time We

love one another still Us missing each

other within the same space and minute

## Visible from Here

Join me in the day

daylight shine

here We're

we are Join me

Well played It

as all that We

witness that we're

boogie boarding?

from an un-seeable

is not visible

the joy is

laughing uncontrollably

laughing I'm

of a powerful

depends on it I'm

Let the objective

upon us You're

here together Here

in the cruel day

can't be as heartless

are each other's

alive Should we go

The swells come in

distance The source

from here but

irrepressible I'm

I'm involuntarily

laughing on the crest

wave Like my life

crying with laughter

I'm crying                uncontrollably You

caught the same           wave a few yards

away We're riding         it in together It's

pure bliss and            breathless adrenaline

all the way in            to shore Then we

charge back out           into the ocean It's

the sun It's salt         and grit and tumultuous

power bigger              than us Bigger

than any of our           small intentions

## Sunshine Bear

What a beautiful day! The sunshine bear is nesting

in its woven sunhat Halo made of loosely woven

twigs The sky bear smiles on a rainbow! The sky bear

lounges on a cloud What a beautiful night!

The moon bear chases a dog chasing a tennis ball

Everything moves a different speed A deep

cold river! A river made of lunar tar! The drop bear

excels at surprise An ambush that begins at blissful

ignorance and ends in unmitigated gore What an

opportunity! What a dark thorny forest! What an icy

apocalypse! The water bear wrings out all its insides

to become a curl of dust A day a century an eon

an oblivion The water bear reconstitutes its desiccated

self when it feels like it and not a moment before

The fire bear forges swords of igneous rock against

a diamond anvil The fire bear scrapes the charcoal grate

The ash bear drags a rake through its ember

garden Smooths out the granular remains

## Just the Other Day

What's left for me here really? Not even a broken

badminton racket Not even an archery target

knocked down by a bear Just the other day

I was sobbing in my chair When was that exactly? Just

the other day I was stripping in the driver's seat

parked at the beach and basking in my sun bucket

On the sand I thought I could fall asleep and have

a dream or two Sun streaming unwillingly through

my eyelids Would I be me when I woke again?

Just the other day I walked to the ocean's edge and filled

an empty shell with water then held it high at the waves'

breaking seam and dumped it out again Hey water

Want to know the odds? One quarter of you droplets

will roll straight back into the sea from the momentum

of the heightened pour One quarter of you will sink

into the sand absorbed One quarter will be reclaimed by a

grasping wave And the last of you will evaporate

straight into the sky So when do I consent to the ascension?

A flock of gulls gathers in a tidal puddle each screeching

the exact same pitch The way they hurl the note out of their

throats how doesn't it tear them open? Just the other day

I saw a plover stand entirely nonchalant just centimeters

from where the seam of breaking waves could reach him

If someone ever sets a wager to stand as close as possible

to the incoming tide where you're disqualified if your feet

get even one molecule of water wet In that case I'd find

a plover and I'd say "I'll stand where that guy is standing!"

## Beautiful Cartography

Don't worry I know I've destroyed

the possibility but please turn towards

me again in our sunny bed as you

wake into the morning We're still

here In hindsight we have a little

time remaining Each a breathing

life existing alongside in such

extravagant blue and green Rewind

These islands we threaded together

into a beautiful cartography A tapestry

of shared reality each word each

hour over years Each care The

tenderness is key Don't worry I have

come to understand that with such

vulnerability each brutality undoes

twenty kindnesses

under I hold it

center walking

ocean All my

one proud one

banderilla staking

that was one

tiny bleeding

volume Don't

the last time

It pulls me

heavy at my heart's

straight into the

tears It was only

colorful flag one

out a victory

too many The

accumulates to

worry We passed

without knowing

## Golden Bonsai

Subsumed remnants of

hovering at the edge

beveled volcanoes

*Be still* The problem

of the mystery

whose gold is blotted

own sheer volume

incremental A critical

the inattention and

the balance Sun rays

one from a daytime

the mesh Each a

extricated from lamé

infringements leaves

palette suddenly

an ancient city Hovel

of a lava plain with

ridging the horizon—

is the scale

A swarming of bees

into black by their

The total reversal is

mass accumulates in

a single bee tips

extracted one by

sky Tweezered from

gold metallic thread

The ratio of thin

behind a graphite

revealed The eyes

refocus to accommodate

charred earth below

to receive the golden

by its inhabitants

riches The soil

until the catacombs

their vaulted ceilings

fold between the

a golden bonsai

branches shimmer

extend in baroque

the darkness The

now hacked open

goblets hoarded

Burial with one's

choked with gold

are sated through

And on the Rorschach

shifting earth and sky

thrives Its gilt

Its black roots

unfolding mirror

## One Grain More

The garden is flowering So many

yellow wax beans cherry tomatoes

I can be beside him picking

the vegetables we grew together

We cut beautiful lettuce leaves

of all different shapes colors textures

with fine orange-handled scissors

and put them in a silver colander

It's possible to wash one leaf at a time

and end up with the world's most

beautiful salad Wild strawberry plants

on our porch offering such tiny

delicate berries full of all the taste

of which they are capable They came

and went but there are still the raspberries

There is still July and the ocean waters

getting warmer even though we're

walking down the far side of the

summer solstice Each day loses

X more minutes of light At some point

it tilts into a landslide an avalanche

of overtaking dark It's a difference

of one grain more of darkness It seems

unfair to drop it on the scale

## A Chambered Vacuole

Light unwoven at the edges The loom

shows around it I keep paring down Soon

nothing will be left Will that make me free

or just poor I swear I hear the waves I hear

the giddiness of starfish The legions line up

to reduce me All the reactive centers All those

handwritten letters sent away from my own

heart Sob in cascades cooling to the dew point I

exhale I breathe in golden light What does this lie

sound like if I listen through it to the generating

source? If I listen through a cataclysmic smile?

What star waste sailed a chambered vacuole to the

cellular edge Sailed smooth in one direction

till it nosed against the outer wall I can't pull

my color back up against gravity There is

no one waiting up for me to make sure I

reach my destination On earth the birds

with golden bellies flit from bush to bush

## Chinese Floating Lanterns

Chinese floating lanterns lift off

into the night sky at the ocean's

edge one at a time they begin

to traverse a great beautiful

distance an arc

way out over the dark

water out into the indistinguishable

dark where the water and the sky

fuse and it's just a black

palette reaching infinitely up

into outer space past the

breath threshold and infinitely

wide past the darkness of

forests you follow

their bright arc you

follow how they trace

light in the sky like

tiny souls they're so

vulnerable they're voyagers

over the planetary waters

over the dark curve of the

earth and when they

snuff out you can't

hear them extinguish the

catch of breath you can't

see the arc of their soft

plummet they're way out

over the water they're a

speck over the water you

can't tell if they are really

gone or if your eyes

couldn't follow them

that far

## Above This Top-Down Labyrinth

Somehow this pressure makes me better than I

was To be present here in the mountains climbing

with my friends I'm alive under the pressure of

the air of the thin altitude of air I have access to all my

senses With wild blueberries implausibly thriving

at the rocky summit So much bounty to enjoy in this

exact moment Inexhaustible Enough for every

one of us And the unseen animals glancing out

from crevices in rock All blunt noses in the air

All blunt noses sorting through the scents We've leapt

above this top-down labyrinth of pain Here at the

knife-blade summit the breeze could knock me over

A thought could level me I left behind

bright estuaries staccatoed with white egrets Cuff-linked

with two mannerly blue herons in their evening

smoking jackets Grey-blue velvet unsmudged by

tears Here one bird who somehow lives at the very

top of this mountain is just ahead of us on the scrubby

trail He issues one note We follow him He flies ahead

He issues one note We follow him He flies ahead

## This High Up

Touch my foot to the island

stepping from the tiny boat

Burns my face I

balance waiting on the swaying

stern Step onto the land

The echoes drift off

the island The echoes

peel back A face

mask off the surface

of the island off the waving

grasses off the beach rocks

Accumulation of boulders Come from

where Their entry here

originated Burns my face

I cut through opaque

textures Past exit strategy

Past runways where solar panels

collect the sun Where solar

panels re-collect Past

sleep Burns my

face I step

onto the pier I touch my foot

to the land to the beach stone

to the driftwood to the sand

Trace the perimeter

then climb on the overgrown

bastion the shattered

pillar Look out

over the open

water Wave

outward into

blue receiving

This high up in the air

This high up

This high

## Time Being

I've already been there and back

and it's over and I

said my piece is it my

peace I said the words in a row

how's that I articulated them

into a microphone the words

carried to the back of the room we had

an hour total to sum it up I had

around three minutes to say my

piece before that we were

out on the open grass and

a box of you in front of us

filled with ashes of you some

parts of you the accuracy

is always a question the

completeness the purity of the

ash I mean how can you

guarantee anyway it was

overcast you could barely

tell that out there was the

enormous Pacific it looked

like just more sky it was

the ocean huge and

engulfing we were there

tiny against all that

panorama and you were tinier

you were a number of ashes inside

a box sitting on some makeshift

green turf your father

lifted the box of your ashes into

a larger urn your wife

put in an envelope no one knows

the contents your mother was sitting

on an outdoor chair crying your

sister behind her was crying

your brother and his wife

your kids having no idea

what was going on anyway

now it's over some dudes

rolled up in a funereal golf cart

they had muddy hiking boots

they knelt down by your urn

it was on a motorized blue fabric

conveyor which they turned on and

lowered you down into a

hole a fairly deep hole the alto hum

of the machinery filled the air

their walkie-talkies crackled from

the golf cart parked nearby we heard

the operator's voice communicate that

some other caskets had been sprayed

and were ready for pick-up "copy"

the fabric conveyor took forever

to lower but also not long enough

I wish you never hit the bottom I wish

there was never a bottom of the

hole and no box and no ashes

on the way here I kept

imagining you might be

on the same plane traveling home

to San Francisco or that I might

see you in the airport

accidentally because Tim it's

the first day of spring today and

it's pretty decent out like 60 degrees

and a good day for riding

your bike and a good day for

a picnic at the beach Em and I

drove to a number of beaches

as your ambassador we wanted

you to be there but we went ahead

for the time being

# Acknowledgments

In "The Elites," the italicized fragments are from John Donne's "Batter my heart, three person'd God" (Holy Sonnet 14). In "Whoso List," the italicized end lines of each stanza are fragments from Sir Thomas Wyatt's Petrarchan sonnet "Whoso List to Hunt." "Golden Bonsai" is in response to Teresita Fernández's exhibition "As Above So Below."

Thank you to the following publications that originally published poems from this book: *White Wall Review* ("Time Being," "Unbalances the Fulcrum"), *Bennington Review* ("Behind Glass," "Prosthetic Mermaid Tails," "Above This Top-Down Labyrinth," "Just the Other Day"), *About Place Journal* ("Whoso List"), *Boog City* ("This Valuable Item," "This High Up"), *Interim: A Journal of Poetry & Poetics* ("Sotto Voce," "Road to Vienna," "Hardened Resins are Called 'Tears'"), *Triggerfish Critical Review* ("Not to Half-Ass It," "Free Market Value," "Dear {Salutation} {Last_Name}," "Maximum Absolution," "Finite Number," "A Chambered Vacuole").

Thanks to these for my safe passage: Drs. Carol and Fred Hochberg, Allison Titus, Michael Tyrell, Donna Stonecipher, Myna Joseph, Sabrina Orah Mark, Yonatan Grad, Caroline Buckee, iLona Mae, Emily Martin, Heather and Gregg Bloom, Mark Levine (and for his incomparable editorial eye).

Eternal gratitude and eternal love: Robin Welte, Jon Woodward, Neil Fidler, Tim Eck.

## KUHL HOUSE POETS